The Chain Breaking Experience: The Gathering of The Prophets and The Prophetesses

Devotional Book

Foreword by

Dr. Monique Rodgers

Compiled by Visionary Coach Ashley Blanshaw & A legendary co-author team

Copyright © 2023 Ashley Blanshaw All rights reserved.
ISBN:
Published by Shooting Stars Publishing House
No parts of this book may be reproduced in any form, stored in a retrieval system, or transmitted in any form by any means-electronic, mechanical, photocopy, recording, or otherwise-without prior written permission of the publisher, except as provided by United States of America copyright law.
Printed in the United States of America

Contents

Introduction..Pg. 4
Foreword...Dr. Monique Rodgers: Pg. 6
Chapter 1...............................Better Days are Coming- Prophet Zinya Gray Pg:11
Chapter 2............................In His Presence-Lady Cheryl Meade: Pg: 17
Chapter 3......................... Devotion of Faith- Prophetess Tara Ware-Jones: Pg. 20
Chapter 4..... The Hand of God-Prophetess Katrina Monique Washington: Pg 27
Chapter 5............ The Battle Ax- Prophetess LeTia Stewart-Kearney: Pg. 37
Chapter 6........ RESET- Pastor Bonnie Smith-Carr: Pg. 44

Introduction

Welcome!!! Welcome to the Chain Breaking Experience: The Gathering of the Prophets and The Prophetess!! Get ready, get ready and get ready because something big is going to happen, something major is going to happen. You will not stay stuck in the circumstances because the chains are being broken. I love that song Break Every Chain by the amazing Tasha Cobbs Leonard. The song says that there is power in the name of Jesus to break every chain. How many believers out there know that there is power in the name of Jesus to break every chain? Every chain that has been holding you bondage, that has been holding you captive and holding you trapped, is going to be broken. No chains or curse is going to stop you from reaching the greater shift that God is going in your life. God is shifting you into a greater position in your life. God is doing something amazing in your life. Just trust and believe. Decree it and declare it that God is going to do it and it will happen. This is your season of excellence. This is your season of breakthrough. This is your season of going from possibility to purpose. This is your season of stepping into the greater calling that God has for you and that he is doing in your life. Something special is about to happen in your life. Isaiah 10:27 says that the Anointing of The Lord destroys every yoke and every yoke and evil curse that the devil has tried to put on you, it is going to be broken and it is going to be destroyed. You are going to break free from the chains and you are going to walk in your miracle. This is the year of chains being broken. Join with these amazing and wonderful authors as they share encouragement about how God is breaking the chains of obstacles and struggles that we were going through.

Foreword

Dr. Monique Rodgers

In these unprecedented times we find that many people in the world are suffering with chains in their mind's chains from past hurts, chains from past and current wounds. There are chains in our lives that need breaking. In this anthology Coach Ashley Blanshaw equips the reader into a new place of understanding the power of deliverance that God brings to his children. This anthology helps to unfold and capture the lives of many women who have gone through and have broken through the chains in their lives and have seen the power of God in full operation and demonstration in their lives. In John 8:36 it declares, "So if the Son sets you free, you will be free indeed." God is our chain breaker. He has come to break you free from every chain and strongly hold your life. He has come to set you free from all the pain in your life and he has come to deliver you out of the bondage that the enemy has tried to put you in for so long. This is your time of freedom. This is your time of deliverance. This is your time of rising and coming out of all that you have been so engraved in from the past years. This is your day of new beginnings. This is your day of redemption. This is your day of freedom. This is your time to press forward into what God has ordained for your life. God has ordained you to be free. That there will be no more chains holding you hostage. No more chains holding you down. No more chains holding you in a place that you cannot get out of. But God is your chain breaker. He has come to bring freedom and deliverance in your life in a way that you have never imagined. So, today as you read this anthology. I pray that there will be freedom in your life. I pray that you will be able to walk in the freedom that Christ has given upon you today that today you will experience the freedom of God and your life in a way that you could never have. imagined before. Freedom is your portion. I know what it is to walk in a place of being in bondage and then experience the freedom of Christ. That is what God wants to do for you today. As you read this book. He wants to break every change in your life and bring you into a place of newfound freedom and Jesus. So, I pray as you read this anthology that chains will begin to immediately break and shatter in your life. That everything that has held you hostage is now leaving your life now in the name of Jesus. I pray that as you read the stories of these women, that there will be something that you can relate to as well and that God will bring complete and total deliverance to your life. Get ready for the chains to break in your life!!!!

Prophet Zinya Gray

Prophet Zinya N. Gray is a native Washingtonian (DC), wife, mother now of 7 grown children, 8 grandchildren. Prophetic ministerial leader and life coach, advocate for family well-being with a passion to bring healing and encouragement to the body of Christ; Organizational Leadership, Building Development, and uses her spiritual gifts and talents to birth and push others to their capacity to be change agents in the Lord. Higher Education: Bachelor's degree in Business Administration. At Ashworth College, Biblical Education graduated with honors at, New Life Hope Seminary School, Now Church attending Ascend Church Ministries as a licensed Minister. Additional ministerial studies and attended a prominent College to further her education. Later received her counseling credentials at (AACC). American Association of Christian Counselors, to counsel families and adults and Pastoral counseling. Pursuing certification credentials for Mental Health Behavior as well. Author: of her personal book called "This Too Shall Pass", Co-Author of 4 books: Honor Thy Mother Anthology:' ' I am My Mother's Daughter", Out of The Cave Experience, When Grace Found Me vol 2 & 3. Media: TV personality Talk show host of two tv broadcast on WBGR Network & WBGR TV, Co-Host on Called With a Purpose every Thursday afternoon @ 1pm Est on WBGR Gospel Network and Co- Host on Reality Take 2 on WBGR Entertainment Saturdays @ 4;30pm Est , Amazon Fire Stick, Roku TV on Sundays @ 7pm est. Senior Executive Accounts Director for WBGR TV Network for Promoting TV & Radio shows. Entrepreneur: with Husband Chef Uncle Big George have several businesses: GZee Productions, LLC a company that creates event venues for family activities & Shows: Zee Beauty Care (zeecarebeauty.com) and Zee Beauty 4 U (etsy.com/shop/ZeeBeauty4U) and online Beauty and Barber products & apparel. GZee Hospitalies is a catering company that we launched early this year! GZee Credit Solutions, (www.ucespp.net/ZGray2) removal of credit issues from clients' credit report that will help boost the client's credit rating. Actress opportunity for movies: Zeke the Awakening Producer KaZaar Coleman, Hopeless Romantic, Keys & Cuffs Producer Michael Steven-Paul (Mikey Jay) more to come! Everything is still a blessing from The Lord! God gets the glory!

Chapter 1

Better Days are Coming

Prophet Zinya Gray

The Lord brought this word to me today for you" Divine Alignment". Reestablish the divine alignment in this season for your life! Alignment to your season, Alignment to your anointing, Alignment to your assignment, Alignment in your health, Alignment in your relationship with people who care for you. Alignment in your job! Alignment in your finances! . God has a perfect timing, a perfect season, a perfect will for your life in HIM. Sometimes we pray and have to wait. Sometimes fasting happens first before the release of HIS Power or HIS Answer! Continue to pray the divine alignment vertically and horizontally lining up with the will of God in your lives. Oh Hallelujah!!! As I hear what the Lord has given me to say to you. This is the year of movement " Better days are coming for you! Psalm 119:17-18 Deal bountifully with thy servant, that I may live, and keep thy word. Open thou mine eyes, that I may behold wondrous things of thy law. Amen!! Thank You Lord ! God has not forgotten you in this season that will propel you and position you into your greatness. Things that you thought would not happen for you, things that will increase you and keep you, to sustain you. It shall manifest, because you prayed and worked hard to get it. Did you know that there is something 10x better that what you have lost, that you will receive double for every measure of affliction you have dealt with in your life. That the Lord wants to prepare for you. How Will

Better Come:- 2 Chronicles 7:13-14 says "If I shut up heaven that there be no rain, or if I command the locusts to devour the land, or if I send pestilence among my people; 14 If my people, which are called by my name, shall humble themselves, and pray, and seek my face, and turn from their wicked ways; then will I hear from heaven, and will forgive their sin, and will heal their land". Here He cause a nation to pray in verse 13 – the world is praying because of the coronavirus. Verse 14 gives the premise prerequisites which are 4 and 3 promises. Remember the message is to the Church and to the World different messages with the same purpose. You've got to believe that your better days are coming. Some of us get stuck in the "glory days" of the past. Because of this, we fail to see that God is doing an awesome thing in our lives today. Well, if you want to see greater things than what you've experienced, then you've got to obey the Lord God who said, "Forget the former things; do not dwell on the past. See, I am doing a new thing! Now it springs up; do you not perceive it? I am making a way in the wilderness and streams in the wasteland. The wild animals honor me, the jackals and the owls, because I provide water in the wilderness and streams in the wasteland, to give drink to my people, my chosen, the people I formed for myself that they may proclaim my praise." Isaiah 43:18-21 Do you want to see the new things that God is doing? If you say yes, then you should stop staying in the past glory that you've had, and start believing that the better days of your life are ahead of you. Here are some reasons to believe why. Because God's mercies are new every morning, your better days are coming! Walk in it each and everyday of your life! Lamentations

3:22-23 tells us, "Through the Lord's mercies we are not consumed, because His compassions fail not. They are new every morning; Great is Your faithfulness." (Lamentations 3:22-23) If you've experienced the Lord's goodness yesterday, then you're going to experience it anew today. And the next day after that Why? It's because God's mercies are "new every morning." You've got to believe that God the Father has a fresh store of mercies available for you every morning that you wake up. Go on and ask the Lord for them. God keeps doing new things, because your better days are coming! Isaiah 43:18-21, said that we should forget the past because He's doing new things. Think about it for a minute. He said those words to the Israelites who knew that in the days of old, God created the universe from nothing, provided deliverance from Egypt using great signs and wonders, parted the sea for His people to cross, rained manna from heaven for bread to eat, healed people of their illnesses, and a lot more. Why would God tell them that? It's because people often get stuck in the glory of the past. God never gets rusty, never gets overworked, never loses fresh ideas, and never loses creativity. If we stay in the past, we won't see the new things that He enjoys doing. Remember, old wineskins burst when new wine is poured in! God isn't finished yet, because your better days are coming! While Jesus' work of atonement is already finished on the cross, God's overall plan isn't finished yet. The Bible says that, "He who has begun a good work in you will complete it until the day of Jesus Christ. Philippians 1:6 This means that being saved by grace through faith was only the beginning line of what God has done and will do to, in, and through us all ! God's not done with you yet, so keep believing for your better days in Him no matter what happens, are coming! Acts 16:25 says, And at midnight Paul and Silas prayed, and sang praises unto God: The praise says we believe the prayer is already answered! It then says "and the prisoners heard them. Somebody needs to hear your prayer and praise in the dark. They need to see that there is hope when things look hopeless. They need to see that you go through darkness differently because we know that God is still in control! Verse 26 says, And suddenly there was a great earthquake, so that the foundations of the prison were shaken. When people see that the people of God can pray and praise with confidence in the midnight hour, the foundation of what holds them in bondage will be shaken! The law of prayer and praise is higher than Murphy's Law is Whatever can go wrong, will go wrong. The truth of the matter is this, it will override the facts so "It's too good to be true" changes into "It's too good not to be true!" What they thought was impossible will be shaken so that they believe all things are possible because they see it working in you, Yes you your better days are coming! The text then says, And immediately all the doors were opened. You can see opened doors that you never noticed before when you look for them. ...And every one's bands were loosed! Strongholds of a poverty and mediocre mindset can be broken if the church will pray in the valley like they do on the mountaintop and do in the darkness of night what they do in the light. Pray and praise like you believe a better day is on the way! As the Lord continues to breath on you to preserve you for such great work, Keep Saying My Better Days Has Come! Walk in it, protest it and allow it to manifest in your life! I speak right now in your life that what ever the Lord is doing right now in this very minute and second of your life! Just say yes Lord, and walk strong in the authority with the strength from the Lord! I decree and declare Your Better Days are already manifesting. No more lack ! No more bondage! No more sleepless nights, and No more tears of sadness! Because you have been praying, because you are expecting new! A New Heart, New Financial Stability, New Business, New Birth, New Revelation, New Health, New Life, A New Word From The Lord, New Relationship that are good for YOU, NEW BOOKS, NEW GIFTS OF THE SPIRIT OF GOD! NEW LEVELS OF EXPANSION That Only God. The Father Can Give! NEW PROTECTION FROM THE LORD, NEW EDUCATION, NEW DEGREES, NEW DECREEING & DECLARING, NEW DWELLING PLACE (HOUSES & LAND) FROM THE LORD! NEW FAVOR!! NEW REWARD!! NEW PLAN FROM THE LORD! NEW PEACE!! NEW PRAYER LIFE! OH HALLELUJAH!

Lady Cheryl Meade

Lady Cheryl Meade was raised in Washington DC and educated in the DC public school system. She is a graduate of McKinley Technical High School, class of 1981. She also attended the University of The District of Columbia where she studied Computer Science and music. Lady Cheryl is a divorcee with 4 children and 8 grandchildren. Lady Cheryl is a devoted mother, grandmother and friend. She is a God fearing woman who loves the lord with all her heart and walks in her calling of Prophet, intercessor and exhorter. Also as a survivor of Domestic Violence, sexual, physical, mental and emotional abuse, Lady Cheryl advocates for women, mental and physical health for people as well as deliverance from mental and spiritual oppression.

Chapter 2

In His Presence

Lady Cheryl Meade

Many people are so busy that they forget to stop and smell the flowers. Nature reminds you of Father God's creation (Psalms 24:1) and when we take time to spend looking at his creation we are reminded that we are his creation as well. Life these days are filled with so many distractions, busyness and all sorts of things that we often times forget to just breathe. I remember when I was so busy working, raising a family, church obligations, football and cheerleading with the kids everyday that I was so tired by the end of the night most times I didn't even pray, just went on to sleep. I was stressed to the max but I loved being outside so I started walking in the park. I noticed how green the grass was and the flowers were beautiful so I said thank you lord for this beauty you created. Then closed my eyes and just started thanking him when I realized I was calm and peaceful. The Bible says that in his presence there is fullness of joy (Psalms 16:11) and I sure felt that in that moment. After that I wanted more so I started taking the time the notice everything around me as I went along my day. The lord says he will keep you in perfect peace if you keep your mind on him (Isaiah 26:3). How do you do that you ask?, well I'll tell you. When you wake up in the morning tell Father God thank you for the breath of life and ask him him what he wants you to do that day. Throughout your day take a minute or two or three or five (lol) to just breathe in and think of something beautiful and for a moment let that be the only thin you think about and remember who created it. Takes long walk or a nice bath and think of all the things he has brought you through. Life can take you through many things and they can be difficult to handle. There a lot of people who are overwhelmed by situations they are in. They have chains of stress, financial woes, family drama, work related stress, just trying to survive with all that baggage can be too much to handle but if you get in Father God's presence those chains can be broken. Matthew 11:30 says "my yoke is easy and my burden is light". When you get in his presence you can allow him take the weight off your shoulders. Being in the true presence of Father God will give you peace, joy and love his presence is everything because nothing else matters in that moment.His presence will give you rest and rejuvenation to help you deal with life's situations. You are his child and he loves you. He sent his son so that we can go into his presence. He wants us to be close to him. Never stop getting in his presence it's good for your mind, body and soul.

Prophetess Tara Ware-Jones

Prophetess Tara Ware-Jones is a servant of Christ, wife, Author, loving mother of four and grandmother of three. Prophetess Tara was born in Millington, TN and now resides in Memphis, TN with her family . She is a minister of the Gospel, Life coach and she also holds a degree in Christian counseling. One of her greatest enjoyments is to see people set free, receive salvation and delivered from the bondages of Satan. She is a prayer warrior at heart and seeks breakthrough for others. She is a rising Apostolic-Prophetic voice that is coming, and a ready weapon of war to set the captives free.

Chapter 3

Devotion of Faith

Prophetess Tara Ware-Jones

Psalm 65: 5-8

⁵ For God alone my soul waits in silence and quietly submits to Him,
For my hope is from Him.. ⁶He only is my rock and my salvation;
My fortress and my defense, I will not be shaken or discouraged.
⁷ On God my salvation and my glory rest; He is my rock of [unyielding] strength, my refuge is in God.⁸ Trust [confidently] in Him at all times, O people;
Pour out your heart before Him.

God is a refuge for us. .

Trusting God sometimes can be hard, and most Christians/Kingdom believers won't admit that but it" s true. Living life according to the bible was never to be perceived as not having any hardship. The bible never told us that as believers that we wouldn't have problems. Before I get started, I just want to share something with you. In 2018 I developed a lump in my right breast and during that time when I noticed the lump. I can remember laying at the foot of my bed and I heard the words *breast cancer*. I immediately rebuke it and spoke back to the voice that I heard. I don't think I shard it with anyone at the time that I heard this voice. And, what happened next was a faith walk. *It was Just me and my God.* I did make an appointment to see the doctor and went to my schedule mammogram appointment. When the test was done what happen next is what I knew was going to change things for me. Once the test was completed the tech went to get the radiologist. Of course, I knew then this was not going to be good news. He said, "Mrs. Jones you have a mass sitting inside of the cyst that is in your breast that we have been monitoring". I said, okay what's next? He said a biopsy. I had the biopsy done a week later and proceeding that was my lumpectomy on my right breast weeks later. After having the lumpectomy I experience encounter from the Lord and He spoke to me very clearly and loving as Father would to His child. Those days where scary and lonely as I awaited the results of the test results, but they were also beautiful. As the Father spoke to me to comfort me in so many ways in the darkest time in my life. He even sent an Angel to a church service I was attending to cover me as I was knelling in church. This Angel laid over me and his wings of many glowing colors covered me as I prayed and cried before the Lord. In the end, THE LORD SHOWED HIMSELF STRONG AND MIGHTY. See women of God with purpose we have to be steadfast even in our darkest hour – even at the final hour. As vessel that will carry *the GLORY AND THE ANOINTING OF GOD* we must be steadfast even when the roaring lion is trying to steal, kill, and destroy our faith in God. GLORY TO THE KING. Let's pray: Father God forgive us for all ours sins known and unknown. Forgive us for not trusting you with everything in our lives. Father, we thank you for rebuking the enemy for our name sake and coming in like a mighty rushing wind to defend us in our time of need. Father, restore our hearts back to you. You are not like man so therefore Father you cannot and will not lie to us in our time of trouble. We bow and posture our hearts before you and ask that you continuously fill us with your presence in our time of sorrow, despair, sadness and feeling of no way out. Father, we honor you and trust you with every word that comes out your mouth. For we know that your words can not return unto you void. Father, we trust you like never before and this time Father, we won't take it back, or pick back up our troubles or problems as we surrender them to you. We thank you for loving us like no one else can. We honor you Lord for who you are, and we trust you with everything in us in Jesus Name I pray Amen.

Prophetess Katrina Monique Washington

Prophetess Katrina Monique Washington Has had a passion for writing all her life; she is a loving and caring daughter, mother, and grandmother and is a faith believer. Katrina has been a healthcare professional since "2001 . Prophetess Katrina is currently a telemetry monitor tech at Vista Medical Center and had the privilege of being a Obstetrician Tech in their New Family Center in Waukegan, IL. She is a minister of the gospel, entrepreneur, creative designer, bridal consultant, outreach minister / coordinator and is also the author of "Thee Black Marker" which has been global since "2019" she has been blessed to be a collaborative author in the #1 best seller UNLOVED "The Leah and Jacob Love Story" in Chapter#7 and CALLED TO INTERCEDE volume 5 "Watchmen On The Wall" in chapter #5 since "2021". She has newly released another book in "2022" called PRAYING ON PURPOSE "Cry Loud and Spare Not" within months of publishing her first book she was interviewed live on the morning news channel 3 WSIL TV NEWS in Cartersville, IL. She has volunteered her services as an Anchor on The People Voice This Week in her Community and has been interviewed on WRLR 98.3 FM RADIO. Which lead to an open door for her to host her very own radio show as a radio show host and producer of the "Single Saved and Successful Inspirational Show" this opportunity unlocked blessings and later in the mouth of three she Illustrated "The Prayer Warriors on Purpose" Intercessor prayer warrior team and establish a prayer hour during the pandemic. She is on a new journey and has joined "Lakes Radio" WLCB 101.5 FM as a radio show host and producer fall of "2022". And will be starting a new inspirational show in January "2023". Katrina has been chosen to do the work of an evangelist, with many more books to be birth, and the help of the Lord; she has served in many compacities in ministry; and often been used in the office of a prophetess and in her less she has always made herself available to bless & reach out in love to the homeless, she is always interceding and advocating as a voice for those who has been silenced, and because of her love in caring for others and her personal experience she has been compelled to save lives, and see others out of the eyes of God, and since "2010" she has made great efforts to be the change she wants to see. Katrina is a Chicago High School graduate, certified nurse assistant, and has successfully completed the medical assistant program, emergency medical technician program and has a food service certificate, she is also FEMA, BLS and HAZMAT certified, she successfully graduated from cosmetology school in "1996" and have a honors degree in Bridal

Consulting, Katrina has many gifts and talents and has invented her own lip balm brand and upon graduating from high school she attended Lincoln University of Jefferson City Mo. Although it was for a short time. God is yet fulfilling his promises towards her and many of her dreams has already manifested full circle. She never expected to be called to ministry even though she was brought up in holiness, but God chose her, and he knew her before she was in her mothers' womb, and he ordained her to be a prophet unto nations according to Jeremiah 1:5. In "2013" she received her initial ministerial fellowship papers through the Midwest district council. while under the umbrella of the honorable Pastor Allan E. Rudd Sr. & First Lady Iris Rudd, she relocated to the Chicagoland area in "2016" and was ordained by the Christian National Church. she has been a participant on the Issachar intercessor prayer line for many years and is presently a member of Indiana Avenue Pentecostal Church of God and was born and raised on a solid foundation while under the leadership of the late Bishop Charles E. Davis, she has been an active member of the Been Through Prayer Line since she has returned to her original church home and have obtained a intercessor certificate, she is now a member of the ministerial alliance of the Illinois District Council, and is honored to be under the new leadership of Bishop Mark A. Moore & First Lady Dr. Shirley Moore at IPC. Katrina loves to read and has broaden her intellect by indulging on her library of books and because of her zeal for spiritual growth she has been fortunate to stand before Kings. Katrina certainly does not look like what she has been through and live to live again and has conquered her fears by walking by faith. She thrives on purpose and trust God for everything, and she have the confidence in knowing that her redeemer lives, and he lives on the inside of her; with his unfailing love he has continue to show out in her life, she is founder of PWOP on clubhouse, Owner of Fresh Start Ministries & Events and have survived battles that many have lost and some has yet to recover, she is elated and truly blessed to still have both of her beloved parents in the land of the living, to share her accomplishments. She has an apostolic and prophetic anointing, studies at Impact University; and is a resident of Lake County, IL.

Daniel 11:32

Chapter 4

The Hand of God

Prophetess Katrina Monique Washington

"For many are called, but few are chosen"-Matthew 22:14

As a woman of God's, I am first a servant, being a spiritual Leader & minister of the gospel. I was chosen to do the work of an evangelist according to 2 Timothy 4:5. In having a relationship with the father I am known as his daughter, who has been privileged to serve God's people. Having a covenant with my savior assures my place in the kingdom, in being that I submit to his will and not my own, I don't even belong to myself. Therefore titles do not define me; for in him i live, and move, and have my being; as certain also of our own poets have said, we the people of God is also his offspring. Which confirms that I am who God's say I am not only because he created me; but because I am in his hands. Many of you may question How do you know when God's hand is upon your life? The answer is that he is the author and finisher of all creation, being that he is the potter and we are the clay we are vessels that he shapes, forms and displays. He illustrates our life journey and knows our ending before our beginning which confirms that he already knew you and I before we was in our mothers womb according to; Jeremiah 1:5. There should be no other place we rather be other than in the hands of God!! Are you a chain breaker? I remember having left the tv on while sleeping as a child one time and in the middle of the night I woke up and in my head; start quoting it; I couldn't tell you what show it was but it was demonic. I began to form my words and repeat what I heard and the Lord stop me before finishing it! That is why we have to be careful what gateways we allow to attach to our children. the enemy tried to make me have a covenant with him by experiences this it was times I felt like something holding me down, and I couldn't talk or scream for help, but I start calling on the name of Jesus and the weight broke off of me. Gifts cometh without repentance even not knowing the power we possess and authority we obtain the name of Jesus is a strong tower the righteous runneth into it and is safe. calling on that name; is what I was taught to do in crisis situations and I learned that he is sure to answers prayers. God is a chain breaker and it is the anointing that destroys the yoke of bondage, have you ever went to a farm and saw a crossbeam on the oxen or animals neck? The purpose of it is to control the direction in which they go, to keep them in line and to stop them from leaving the pack!Matthew 11:28-30 says come unto me, all ye that labour and are heavy laden, and I will give you rest. Take my yoke upon you, and learn of me; for I am meek lowly in heart: and ye shall find rest unto your souls, for my yoke is easy, and my burden is light! If you go back and read the history you will understand that repentance was necessary in their deliverance, it reveals Jesus speaking and praying to the father himself and summons the multitude. To break it is to interrupt the process of a binding state; It is spring-fourth, breakout, let go, to be delivered, redeemed and captured. in the verse you see how flesh will hinder you from your break through being carnal minded will limit your ability to break free and the realm of darkness will hold you captive to boundaries but in being spiritual minded will bring light in every in situation. Because who the son set free is free indeed. remember Paul and Salis prayed and sang praises unto God at midnight while in prison; and suddenly a earthquake took place, the foundations was even shaken and immediately the doors and the bands was loosed. In other words they gave God the praise in the middle of the dilemma, they didn't wait until they got out of the situation but they reverence God as their redeemer in advance, they broke up the follow ground because they honored God as their savior, although they could have ran seeing that the masses of prison was destroyed! The fear of God came upon the prison guards and they began to bow, when the light sprang in because they recognized the power that was invested in Paul and ask what must they do to be saved. Growing up in church was enjoyable, I wanted to go, I didn't have to be prompt or primed! I had an aunt that raised me up in church; who was an excellent display of holiness, but I never gave ministry a 1st or 2nd thought; Being that my parents had not yet surrendered, I was allowed to participate in activities outside of the church. I loved the tv show fame and I was good at dancing, and became not only a cheerleader, but a coach of my own cheerleader team in elementary school at the age of only 10 and was very popular. Dancing was in my bones, I was on my local park district dance team in competitions and, not to mention I love me some Michael Jackson to the point I was in one of his fan clubs, I wore a glitter glove to school and put a Shirley temple girl in front of my hair to reflect him, I even went as far as being in the spotlight by dancing and performing in talent shows and birthday parties. If I went to the party and it was dead I was what they called the hype person that influenced others to dance. And As much as I loved to dance I am grateful to say I never had a desire to dance on a pole, I had a sassy mouth and curse like a sailor but now I am a curse breaker because God hand was upon my life! Although I had a loving family raised by both of my parents, it came to a point that I felt like something was missing, like I didn't belong and one day I contemplated suicide and tried to cut my wrist when I was around 12, but it didn't work because God blocked It!! I longed to become a nurse, after nursing on my dad after he had a fall; we was racing one day coming from the candy store; but the heel of his stacks broke and he was scarred up, but he was still my hero, I was around 8 or 9 when a doberman pinscher tried to attack me within only 2 feet! He was barking in my face but my dad immediately reach back as far as could and bust the dog in his head with a ice cold beer can. He was my protector when we took walks he held my hand so tight that it was red, but one day My dad wasn't there but God made a way for my escape when I was cornered by a guy in the hallway of a building while going to visit one of my aunts; when I was only 6 years old I was devastated, but God led me to squeeze through the broken plexi glass window that separated the door and I began to run for my life! My senior year in high school was awesome so I thought: after all I was elected "Lady Orr" during prom! but the day of graduation practice came; I went to load the bus and my name wasn't on the list! It was embarrassing, shouldn't I have had a fair warning, my thoughts of how my family was going to respond with disappointment because their expectations were set so high! I had already been accepted at Lincoln university, I had a lead part in the school chorus for the ceremony and to find out school fees was not only an issue, but I was missing a half of credit, and had to graduate from summer school! I wasn't aware that I had a voice so No one never knew that I was Sexually assaulted in my youth and in college; emotional scars and trauma from unhealthy relationships lead me to have low-self esteem, babies out of wedlock and I was full of bitterness by the age of 35 I was an unwed mother of 4, physically abused by a man I dated his hands felt like a brick Brillo pad as he slapped my face for no reason; my first response was to slap him back, and when I tempted to before I knew it he did it again, my face was stinging, I just knew it was swollen, so my second response was to jump out of the car while he was driving but as I went to open the door he snatched me back in! It was a time that I was homeless but prideful, was engaged and in a relationship for 7-years with a man that was on drugs but never was introduced to it! Rejection has been at its all-time high, and at one point in my life; Doctors told me I may die. but to God be the glory his plans for me never changed and he has proven himself to me on many occasions, through hard trials and tribulation I am determined to walk with Jesus, and as he continue to strengthen, grace me and use me I will stay on the wall and adhere to the call. I am a true worshipper, dreamer and faith walker that has been blessed to have an prophetic and apostolic anointing and Today I can stand and have a answer for every man not because of any heroic acts of my own but because of God's grace it is sufficient for me, I am save, sanctified, Holy Ghost filled a water baptize according to Acts 2:38. He chose me, he preserved me for such a time as this. I am no longer a slave to sin but the righteousness of god, I am not bound but I am free, I am not cursed but I am blessed, I am not a victim but a victor, no longer a failure but I am faithful, I am not abandon but adopted, I am not a loser, but I am a winner, I am not sick, because by his stripes I am already healed, I am no longer naïve, but I am a success. I decree and declare that the devil is defeated and God is exalted. The breaker is here; and if God be for you he is more than the whole world against you! For the breaker is come up before them: they have broken up, and have passed through the gate, and are gone out by it: and their king shall pass before them, and the Lord on the head of them, remember the devil can't curse what God has already blessed, so let God be God and trust him because there shall be glory after this! I want to encourage you because of the mandate. on your life is bigger than you! Maybe you weren't ordained by man, but you were chosen by God. So, will you stand in the breach now? Leah wasn't chosen by Jacob but was chosen by God to be a mother of nations, so don't you allow fear of people, your past or your circumstances to hinder you from fulfilling your purpose. Remember the promise of our four fathers, is yes and amen. Often times you may have to encourage yourself like David and praise your way out, although he was just a little shepherd boy, God's hand was upon him and he choose David one day to become a king; for Promotion cometh neither from the east, nor the west, nor from the south. But God is the judge: he putteth down one, and setteth up another. For in the hand of the lord there is a cup, and the wine is red; it is full of mixture; and he poureth out of the same: but the dregs thereof, all the wicked of the earth shall wring them out and drink them. God will make your name great! Not because you deserve it but because he is great, and he has a plan to prosper you. We have to come realization that The gathering of the prophets is necessary because of the time we are in, and God is holding us all accountable to be obedient and respond quickly and be intentional about adhering to the clarion call because somebody life is predicated on our delivery!! I encourage you to speak life into every situation, and know that it is a purpose for your pain and if god brought you to it, he will bring you through it because his the hand is on your life! I am just a willing vessel that want to be used by God, that he may get the glory out of my life; I have been through too much not to worship him; it took years for me to realize I had gifts because I wasn't in the proper position; but when we humble myself; God honored my posture of humility; God may use you through dreams, people, signs and or real-life experiences and most of the time when you face situations, he is preparing you for greatness. It may not look good, feel good or smell good; but you must know the power that you possess when his name is applied, because his name is above every name. unfortunately in many cases we give the enemy too much credit and instead of telling him how big our God is we have a pity party which gives the enemy access to speak into your ear gates and make you feel inferior; but you must keep on the full armor of God and be strong in the Lord and in the power of his might, According to Ephesians 6:10. Standing against the wiles of the devil; disrupts hells plans to deceive you. Making commands and being in a covenant with the father, having a perpetual prayer and fasting life enables you to fight against the flesh and defeat the kingdom of darkness; you will bind and loose those things on earth as it is in heaven. According to Matthew 18:18. Speak to mountains and they shall be moved, and the enemy will have to stand down. Knowing your battles is vital in your faith walk we must believe that the same power that raise Jesus from the dead is the same power that inside of you. There hath no temptation taken you but such as is common to man: but God is faithful who will not suffer you to be tempted above that ye are able; but will with the temptation also make a way to escape, that ye may be able to bear it. You are not a mistake, but you are a chosen generation, a royal priesthood, an holy nation, a peculiar people; that ye should shew forth the praises of him who hath called you out of darkness into his marvelous light. Therefore; you are daughters and sons of light and day, not darkness and night. Your dreams, signs and your personal experience is relevant to your next level you will learned how to discern what it is right wrong and good and evil; when you hearken unto God's voice, he will speak through you, that is why we must be spiritually incline and have an ear to hear so that you may hear him clearly and apply it so your delivery may be effective. "THEY SHALL STILL BRING FORTH FRUIT IN OLD AGE; THEY SHALL BE FAT AND FLOURISHING"- PSALM 92:14

Prophetess LeTia Stewart-Kearney

Prophetess LetTia Myesha Stewart-Kearney is a true example of a woman of Wisdom & Grace. LeTia Myesha is a faithful servant to the Lord and Savior Jesus Christ for over 38 years since the age of 7 years old. She is a loving and devoted wife, a dedicated mother, spiritual mother, and a mentor. As she walks alongside her husband always willing to assist in any capacity. She is a fun loving and balanced woman of God. She is not one that will just sit to be waited on; she will help wherever help is needed. God has blessed her with the gift of administration which has afforded her the ability to be an outstanding executive, visionary, delegator, pusher, and an assistant and her commitment to excellence has encouraged many brothers and sisters in Christ Jesus. As she walks in the wisdom and favor of God, she has been given the ability to multitask in several capacities as a great asset to the body of Christ. LeTia Myesha special interest focuses on the ethical principles of God though edification and building the Kingdom System of God through the holy ghost. By establishing a safe haven and promoting positive thinking not only in thoughts but in actions believing and living in an environment of quality that generates for this generation and generations after. As a result, The Prayer Well Ministries was birth that produce; 3 Days of Declaration, 5 Days of Fasting & Prayer (I'm Grace For It), Level Up Bible Study, "GAP" (Gods Anointed & Appointed Pourers) Leadership, Beloved Queens Mentorship, and serving as an Overseer/Leader that allows the greater level of maturity to be embodied. These alliances are to motivate a strategic plan for discipline, consistency, development, and much more in the lives of God's people for His Kingdom. She is a vessel used by God for much needed aspiration and as a Fire ignitor of God to kindle the dreams and visions for both spiritual and natural growth. LeTia Myesha has stood the test of times and she is still evolving but her posture and position has certified her by Adonai to make a difference in the Grace that has been given unto her to execute. She takes pleasure in the family structure, therefore spending time with her husband William and five children Daughters, Kiranya, Ka'Mira, Karis, (Bonus Babies) Aaliyah, Jacob, (Grandsons) Josiah and Ronald is a significant part of her life. As well as my extended sons, daughter, mentees and spiritual children. She leaves this with us; Be honest to Be Help!!! God can't heal what we are not willing to expose and God can't deliver to you what He has divinely prepared for you. If you are not willing to be honest, to be posture, to get in position to execute what you have been ordained, appoint, anointed and born in this world for. Peace & Blessing,

LeTia Stewart-Kearney

Chapter 5

The Battle Ax

Prophetess LeTia Stewart-Kearney

"You are My battle-ax and weapons of war: For with you I will break the nation in pieces; With you I will destroy kingdoms;"
Jeremiah 51:20 NKJV

We are living in a time where we want more of what seems to be gratifying the expectations of our needs and desires rather than securing the administration of our kingdom influence. Sons of God we don't want the battle ax of God to break what we have been in chains (linked up) to for so long. We would rather minister in song, preach, prophecy, teach, serve, praise and much more in fetters and handcuffs, being bound to the mentality of a mind institution and with an unhealed heart. Then seek the seeker, the chain breaker that has the ability and the right weapons to set us prisoners free. The one that can reveal (to heal) and release (to liberate) unloosing us into a place of freedom. (True Freedom In Him) Breaking separates and smashes (shatter, crack, disintegrate) into pieces what has kept us in lifetime and lifestyles of trauma/ trauma bond and living in a dysfunctional life of confusion hindering us from the fullness of God's deliverance. Freedom releases us to understand that the battle ax has come to rescue us, but also posture and position us into a place of unquestionable freedom. (John 8:36 amp So if the Son makes you free, then you are unquestionably free) Where there is no breaking there is no exposer (transparency-inward clarity) assessment within self-wanting to be free. The Battle Ax (God)~El-gibbor the ("Mighty God") is our weapon of war, that has the assignment to fight for us and prepare us into a place that has already been predestined for us to fulfill our Mission and life ordained assignment on this life's journey. Let the battle ax of God demolish what has been trying to demolish you for seconds, minutes, hours, days, weeks, months, and years. Allowing Him to work will teach you how concerned He is about youHis (Son/Daughter). He comes to break in and off you what has been a stronghold not to break you to be broken but to break you to free you. It authorizes you to see that operating in areas of your life chained up is no benefit to you but a death sentence to your seed not to grow and flourish in the living water of God. I don't care how gran or great men may tell you or you may tell yourself you are. Being bound limits (retrains, cap, places a limit on) you to a limitless (boundless, infinite, endless never ending) God. Chainless: Sons of God producing comes when your ground has been broken and destroyed letting go and trusting a trusted dependable God to flow in every area of your life. Positioning you in a secure and firm place in the foundation of the Father. See Sons of God many want the glory but not the process of the breakout to breakthrough. Process requires you to act upon (come out of what has been familiar and a habit to you) and requests you to (show up differently~ what worked before is no later efficient). The Fathers heart is set on disentangling you. God is saying He cannot use you to break up/off (being a deliver) until you chose to be broken in me the great deliverer of deliverers. We cannot commission (in power and in authority)effectively from a place that we are not free in, because than we are becoming wonder and not vessels of the healer that has healed. I say give permission and let the God of the battle ax break what has come to break and chain you. Be the sacrifice to the end of the (fill in the blank) because broken chains demonstrate (movement) the sound of freedom and releases (an open mouth expression)the sound of victory. Prayer Father, I (your name) want to honor and love on you before there is any request. Thank you for saving me from me. Thank you for being kind, loving, faithful, intentional, and patient with me. I am grateful that you never left me where you found me, and you remain in the place of open arms for me to come into a place of safety. I thank you for being the battle ax that comes to break and free me out of any place within me that has me bound into a place of unexplainable freedom in you. Father if there are any chains that I am aware and unaware of I ask that you reveal them to me and when you reveal I will follow your instructions to be free. You said that I am your weapon of war, but I first must understand that I cannot be a weapon of demise to the war that you want to remove and free me from that's within me. I desire to be used by you and for you master. I want to be a weapon of great surprise being your best kept secret that breaks and destroys; family dysfunction, fear, abuse (physical, emotional, or sexual), and anger, addictions, unforgiveness, poverty, deception, depression, lying, orphan spirits, pride, spirits of disorders, infirmity, impurity and more. Being useful in your hands and not a hinderance to the flow of your kingdom. So Father break the chains off me and I announce and come out of agreement that I do not link the chains back together again to make a excuses not to be free. Adonai I declare and decree that I will and I can be and remain free and I will follow you because I understand you called and chosen me. In Jesus Name Amen

Pastor Bonnie Smith-Carr

Pastor Bonnie B. Carr is a native of Waterbury, Connecticut who currently resides in the state of Southern Maryland. Pastor Carr is married to Michael Carr and has 3 children, James, Mikael, and Taniya. Pastor Carr received Christ at an early age and has been proclaiming the Word of God ever since. Pastor Carr was educated in the public schools of Waterbury, Connecticut and graduated from Wilby High School in 1984. Pastor Carr holds an associate degree in Applied Science from Briarwood College in which she majored in Dental Assisting/Administrative Assisting. She also graduated with honors from Ashworth College and majored in Medical Billing and Coding in which she is a member of the International Honor Society DELTA EPSILON TAU by election at the Ashworth College Alpha of Georgia. To enhance her gift of prophecy she completed a certificate program from Another Touch of Glory Ministries/ School of the Prophets. Pastor Carr pursued her undergraduate education at Newburgh Theological Seminary and College of the Bible and received her Bachelor of Arts Degree in Christian Counseling in December 2015. Pastor Carr also received her graduate education at Newburgh Theological Seminary and College of the Bible and received her Master of Arts Degree in Christian Counseling on June 5, 202. Pastor Carr received certificates in Youth & Adult Mental Health First Aid USA. Pastor Carr is the author and self-publisher of "And Now I See, What Are You Hiding Under Your Makeup?" You can find her book on Amazon.com and it is available in the Charles County Public Library. She is a contributing Author of the book "Determined to Succeed" by Author Dr. Caretha Crawford and a writer for Hidden Strengths Ministry Newsletter. Pastor Carr has been interviewed on the 1OnONE with Damon Davis Program to discuss her book which aired on The IMPACT and TCT Network Channel on December 8, 2017.Through her new ministry, she is the founder of Bonnie Carr Ministries, LLC "No Negative Talk". April 2017, Bonnie Carr Ministries LLC entered Apostolic Covenant with Alpha & Omega Covenant Fellowship (Baltimore, MD) under the direction of Apostle Benson Kornegay for the advancement of the kingdom of God. She lives out her passion for ministering to women of various ages and ethnic background to encourage, support and empower women to let them know that they are fearfully and wonderfully made and no longer must hide their emotions under their makeup. Pastor Carr also has a lipstick line called bcm Cosmetics. Pastor Carr received her Certificate of Ordination as a Minister on September 29, 2018, from True Foundation Apostolic Ministries under the direction of Bishop Eric Zimmerman. Pastor Carr also started New Breath of Life Covenant Ministries, Inc. in which she received her Certificate of Ordination as a Pastor and her husband Michael Carr as Elder from Ebenezer International Covenant Fellowship/Certificate of Affiliation Certificate on June 26, 2021. Pastor Carr is a stay-at-home mom, part time substitute teacher and faithfully volunteered at her daughter's school in which she was a part of the Reading Buddy program to assist students with reading and comprehension. Through her Bonnie Carr ministries, she also has partnered with Charles County Social Services Outreach Program to help assist families in need. Through her Bonnie Carr Ministries, she has yearly Women Empowerment Conferences and proceeds are donated to the women/families in need in Charles County. Pastor Carr has spoken at various schools to students in reference to bullying, low self-esteem, and depression. Pastor Carr enjoys traveling, singing, baking, completing cross word puzzles, shopping, musical plays, and watching good movies. Interest: Ministering to women and teenagers that have a background of abuse and neglect, low self-esteem, bullying, and depression. Favorite Scripture: Proverbs 3:5-6 Trust in the Lord with all thine heart; and lean not unto your own understanding. In all thy ways acknowledge him, and he shall direct thy paths.

Chapter 6

RESET

Pastor Bonnie Smith-Carr

I just want to tell you that it's time to RESET! According to the Webster dictionary reset means to "set again" or "differently". It's time to change your mindset and do things differently. I know you may feel that you messed up, but you have time to make a "U-TURN". Don't worry about what people say, you know why? Because you don't need anyone's APPROVAL!! God is the only one that approves what YOU are doing. It's time to RESET. It's time to get your joy and peace back. Focus on what God has you to do to reach your destiny. Reset your mind. See the enemy wants your mind. Your mind is the battlefield, and you must speak to that nasty devil and say, "NO NOT TODAY". I'm getting my peace back! You must stop having a Negative Mentality. Speak Life into yourself. Speak Life into your situation. The Bible says in Proverbs 18:21 Death and Life are in the power of the tongue, And those who love it will eat its fruit. You see words kill and words give life. Amen. So, stop saying, I'm not good enough, I'm too fat, I'm too skinny, I'm broke, I'm ugly, I'm never going to get married, and I'll never get that job. You get my point. You have the power to break those generational curses IN JESUS NAME. This is something to rejoice about! Hallelujah. The Bible says in Hebrews 12: 1 NIV Therefore, since we are surrounded by such a great cloud of witnesses, let us throw off everything that hinders and the sin that so easily entangles, and let us run with perseverance the race marked out for us. The NKJ version says, "lay aside every weight." Too often we go around carrying unnecessary burdens which causes us to feel bad. Your carrying loads that are not yours to carry, such as guilt, shame, bitterness, hurt, unforgiveness, fear, anger, worrying, hopelessness, and regrets. You're walking around with so many negative thoughts in your head, almost like a time bomb waiting to explode. The good news is that the Lord came to bear our burdens. The Bible says in Psalm 55:22 Cast your cares on the Lord and he will sustain you; he will never let the righteous be shaken. Quit walking around as victims and walk as VICTORS!! Be free today. Whom the son sets free is free indeed. Reset and take authority over those negative thoughts. ("i.e.," guilt, bitterness, hurt, abuse, etc.) IN JESUS NAME. In order to reset, you must KILL it at the root. You can't let it take root in your hearts. If you don't KILL it at the root, it will grow back. LET IT GO. It's time to give the bill of divorcement to those spirits. Forgive yourself. Forgiveness is for you. There is nothing that you have done in your past that is too much for the mercy of God. Move forward today. Don't give up in this season. You are redeemed. Shake it off and remember, you are a winner in Gods eyes. It's time to RESET.

Made in the USA
Middletown, DE
15 April 2023